Hey Bear Ho Bear

With Lila Liverwort

and Herman the Ermine

Written by Stacy Studebaker

Illustrated by Kay Underwood

Sense of Place Press - P.O. Box 970, Kodiak Alaska 99615

Sense of Place Press
P.O. Box 970
Kodiak, AK 99615

Seventh Printing

Printed in China by Everbest Printing Investment Co. Ltd.
through **Alaska Print Brokers**
Library of Congress Catalog Card Number - 2012951953

ISBN 978-1578335916
Layout and graphic design by Stacy Studebaker
All illustrations by Kay Underwood

Hello, I'm Lila Liverwort
Some stories I will share
About how people can behave
To be more bear aware

When you're hiking in the woods and in the bushes to one side
You hear a scary noise out there that makes you want to hide
Your heartbeat skips to double and your senses come aware
Is it a fox, a deer, a squirrel, a weasel or a bear?

When you're going on an outing in the land of Bear Country
You need to have an attitude to proceed respectfully
For after all the bears were there before we came along
So when you're hiking through you need to sing this little song

HEY BEAR HO BEAR what are you gonna do?
I'm here, you're there, I'm just passing through
HEY BEAR HO BEAR it's such a lovely day
This is your land, I understand
So I'll be on my way

When you're looking for a campsite or a place to spend the night
Be sure you're off the bear trail or you might get quite a fright
Keep your food packed up and hidden and away from where you sleep
Or a hungry bear might think that you are something good to eat!

When you're in your tent at night and woken up from peaceful dreams
And you hear strange sounds outside the tent that make you want to scream
Compose yourself amidst the thuds, the thumps, and all the snuffling
And sing this song to whatever it is so you can send it shuffling.

HEY BEAR HO BEAR what are you gonna do?
I'm here, you're there, I'm just passing through
HEY BEAR HO BEAR it's such a lovely day
This is your land, I understand
So I'll be on my way

When you're standing in a stream by your favorite fishing hole
And you fling that fly expertly with your favorite fishing pole
Suddenly you hear a SPLASH and come up face to face
With a mama bear and hungry cubs who want to take your place

So very slowly you reel in and back yourself away
You never run and never scream but keep your cool that day
You grab your backpack on the way and take your fish along
And all the while in a calm voice you sing this little song.

H

HEY BEAR HO BEAR what are you gonna do?
I'm here, you're there, I'm just passing through
HEY BEAR HO BEAR it's such a lovely day
This is your land, I understand
So I'll be on my way

Our trash and garbage is locked up inside the shed or shop
Until we take it to the dumpster and fasten down the top
Special dumpsters are designed to keep the brown bears out
We only have to do our part, that's what it's all about

HEY BEAR HO BEAR what are you gonna do?
I'm here, you're there, I'm just passing through
HEY BEAR HO BEAR it's such a lovely day
This is your land, I understand
So I'll be on my way

In our town we do our best to keep our brown bears wild
We fenced around our landfill so we keep them way outside
If bears eat garbage they can't stop and may become a pest
They'll try to eat a lot of things their stomachs can't digest

Forests, tundra, beaches, lakes - rivers, streams and bogs
Mountains, meadows, ponds and swamps - even under logs
Lots of wild food choices there for every hungry bear
No need for them to eat our trash if we are more aware

But if they break into your house they'll make a huge big mess
While searching for some food to eat they'd cause you much distress
They'll break into your cupboards and forage through your fridge
For anything that's edible including scones and porridge

Human food is good for us but never good for bears
If by mistake they get too much they might not fancy theirs
They get in trouble eating trash or breaking down our door
And might end up as one big rug on someone's wall or floor

Like us, our bears are omnivores that eat all kinds of things
They prowl around and taste and smell and eat what nature brings
With long strong claws they dig and scratch and eat what seems delicious
They chase and pounce on moving prey including crabs and fishes

Goosetongue
Blueberry
Lingonberry
Salmonberry
Sedge
Lupine
Red Elderberry
Horsetail
Nettle
Cow Parsnip

Brown bears eat a lot of food that seasonally varies
In fall they munch most notably on salmon and on berries
Spring and summer favorites are goosetongue, roots and sedges
Plus clams and bugs and many things that wash up on the beaches

They also feast on larger things that die and drift to shore
Like seals and whales and sea lions and things from the sea floor
One whale can feed a lot of bears who have to take their turns
With other local scavengers like gulls and fox and worms

On mountain ridges bears have walked along their bruin highways
For centuries they've used these trails for berry eating forays
So deeply worn are their big tracks it really is amazing
How every bear could place their paws so carefully while grazing

Or maybe it's a game for them to walk in those big tracks
Like us when we walk down the street and do not step on cracks
With mama bear out in the front with such a lengthy stride
The cubs that follow have to stretch and make their paces wide

At night they like to make a bed and sleep under the stars
And maybe dream of far off worlds like Jupiter or Mars
They sometimes line their bed with leaves to make it soft and warm
And snuggle down on chilly nights or curl up in a storm

H

From lack of food they will retreat from cold and icy weather
In mountain dens they dig or find somewhere amidst the heather
Alder, willows, rocks and cliffs may offer more protection
For mama bear to have her cubs and give them much affection

Seeing bears is such a thrill, we watch them from a distance
We give them lots of space and room and strive for coexistence
A clean environment for the bears is certainly a plus
A place that's good for bears to live is also good for us!

Hey Bear Ho Bear what are you gonna do?
I'm here, you're there, I'm just passing through
Hey Bear Ho Bear it's such a lovely day
This is your land, I understand
So I'll be on my way

The Creators of the book

Photo by John Studebaker

Stacy Studebaker has lived in bear country most of her adult life. She worked in Yosemite National Park right after college in 1971 and later migrated to Alaska working for the National Park Service in Glacier Bay and Katmai National Parks. After earning a Master's degree in Science Teaching and Environmental Education, she moved to Kodiak Island which has been her home since 1980. As one of Kodiak's leading naturalists, she has worked as a science teacher, botanist, whale skeleton reconstructor, musician, artist and photographer. As host, "Lila Liverwort", Stacy coproduced "My Green Earth" an award-winning, weekly radio show about the environment that aired throughout Alaska and the U.S. In 2010, she published "Wildflowers and Other Plant Life of the Kodiak Archipelago" a field guide for the flora of Kodiak and southcentral Alaska. In 2011, Stacy was awarded the Celia Hunter Award by the Alaska Conservation Foundation for her lifetime of volunteer conservation work.

Photo by Arin Underwood

Since 1978, Kay Underwood has fished commercially for salmon with her husband and four children at their set net site on Kodiak Island in the heart of bear country. She has illustrated a series of children's science books for Northword Press of Minnesota and the BBC featured her artwork for a documentary on wild salmon. Her vibrant artwork is used by Alaskan businesses, graces the walls of many Alaskan homes, and illustrates her well-known note cards. She has always been passionate about science and art, and loves the opportunity to illustrate for children. By blending art and science she strives to educate people about the natural world around us.

This book and its beautiful illustrations demonstrate respectful human behavior around bears in urban and wild settings. Stacy and Kay hope to instill a better understanding of brown bears as complex, sensitive, and intelligent creatures while at the same time foster an appreciation for the biodiversity and wonder of the natural world. We hope our contribution will promote a more peaceful coexistence between bears and humans.

Special thanks to the Kodiak Unified Bear Subcommittee (KUBS), The Kodiak National Wildlife Refuge, Bill Leacock, Bill Pyle, Gary Wheeler, Tonya Brockman, Larry Van Daele, Mike Sirofchuck, the Underwood family, Vered Mares, Todd Communications, Alaska Print Brokers, Kodiak College, and Norstar Color.